For Katherine, Luke, and
Sienna, who bring the
magic to life.
- C.L.K.

To Davis and Tobin,
for all the late nights
and long bedtimes.
- G.L.M.

Published by Shasta Blue Press LLC in 2020.

Written by Christy Laakmann Kaupinen and Gayle Laakmann McDowell.
Illustrations compiled and edited by Christy Laakmann Kaupinen from works by a global
collection of graphic artists. Bedtime Bunny, Rabbit King, and other bunny characters
designed by Ahmad Imam Rozay. Special thanks to Laura Leszcynski, Erin Chinnock, and
Danielle Fisher for their thoughtful edits and guidance.

ISBN 978-1-7342779-1-3

10 9 8 7 6 5 4 3 2

Printed in China

The BEDTIME BUNNY

by Christy Laakmann Kaupinen & Gayle Laakmann McDowell

SHASTA BLUE PRESS

Deep in the enchanted woods
where surly oak trees grow,
the magic creatures gathered as
their king paced to and fro.

"This problem's getting out of hand!"
the royal rabbit said.
"We cannot do our jobs without
the children in their beds!"

"The **tooth fairy** is trapped indoors,

the **unicorns** won't fly,

the leprechauns can't find their gold,

and the **dragons** are going to cry!"

All the creatures of the kingdom
were hiding out of sight
because their powers would be lost
if spotted in the night.

Coast to coast, around the world,
kids stayed up much too late.

But at the house on Red Fox Lane
things were by far the worst.

Red Fox Ln

The children had their days and nights
just about reversed!

The girl jumped rope
all through the night

while the boy
made Doggie bark.

And now their newest baby born
would wake when it was dark.

So the king asked his daughter,
"Would you go check for me?
Make sure the children are in bed
so our creatures can fly free?"

"But I've never left these woods!"
the little bunny cried.
"How will I get to Red Fox Lane?
How will I get inside?"

The rabbit king scratched his chin,
his mind was deep in thought...

"Use the **magic carrot**," he said,

"that's in their flowerpot!"

"Tonight when the sun goes down
and bedtime's on the clock,
the carrot's smell will lead you there;
its magic will turn the lock."

The king wrapped her in a cloak
to keep her warm and hidden.

And that night the little bunny
set out on her mission.

She hopped along the moonlit path,
her nose tipped in the night,

following that sweet spring smell
'til the house was in her sight.

With her paws, the bunny plucked the carrot from the ground.

In a flash the lock popped open with just the faintest sound.

Through the door and up the stairs as quick as she could creep...

She peeked into
the children's rooms
and found them all asleep.

She was tired from her journey
but her heart was filled with pride,
so she mustered all her powers
and left a gift inside.

The bunny dashed back through the woods
and called out far and near:

"They're all asleep! Their eyes are shut!

Come out, the **coast is clear!**"

When she told her friends about
the house where she had hopped,
they all wanted to find their own
families to adopt.

Now each night they sniff the air,
their chins out past their toes,
hoping for the scent of carrot
to fill their bunny nose.

25

If you want your very own
here's what you need to do:

Leave out a special carrot with
your name and bedtime too.

Your Bedtime Bunny will pick it up
and keep it in their care,
And in its place, your friend will leave
a sign that they've been there.

Then every night they'll
come to check
that you are
tucked in tight.

So if you're up
when bedtime's passed,
you'll give them
quite a fright.

On special days, or just because,
they'll leave a note or treat
but their magic is still growing
so gifts are quite a feat.

They will never let you see them-
these bunnies are shy, you see.
But right at dusk, some say they've seen...

a **tail** behind a tree.

FAQs

How can our family get our own Bedtime Bunny?

Write your names and bedtimes on the back of the carrot included in your book, then leave it by your front door. Once you're asleep, a Bedtime Bunny will come hopping and leave something special for you. After that, your bunny will continue to hop to your house each night after bedtime.

How often will the Bedtime Bunny leave something?

In the beginning, the bunny leaves something very often - sometimes every night - so you know he or she has been there. After a while, it might be just on special occasions like a birthday, and sometimes "just because" as a surprise! This keeps it fun and exciting, and helps to remind you that the bunny is always hopping, every single night.

What will my Bedtime Bunny leave?

Every bunny is different. Most of the bunnies are very young, so their magic is not strong enough to leave large presents very often. Some bunnies prefer to leave things like notes and stickers, and others leave sweet treats and small toys from time to time.

Please share your adventures with us on Facebook & Instagram @thebedtimebunny!
For more fun, look for the carrot hiding on every page of this book!
Find more FAQs and other goodies at thebedtimebunny.com.